SOUTH AFRICA

A Quick Guide to Cape Town & Jo'burg

The intent of the author is to offer general information on travel to South Africa. The
author assumes no responsibility for the actions of the reader.

Cover Model: Kishema Pendu Malik
Cover Design: Nadine C. Duncan
Interior Design: Nadine C. Duncan

ISBN: 979-8-9889182-2-6
ISBN: 979-8-9889182-3-3 (eBook)

2nd Edition, August 2023
Travel Guide Series, Volume IX
Printed in the United States of America

Published in the United States by:
Traveling Black Women™
Grace Royal International, LLC
Atlanta, GA 30316

www.travelingblackwomen.com

Diary of a Traveling Black Woman:
A Guide to International Travel

"Mini Travel Guide Series"
Volume IX - South Africa

South Africa:
A Quick Guide to Cape Town & Jo'Burg

Kishema Pendu Malik

The Traveling Black Women Network
Grace Royal International, LLC
Atlanta, GA

Diary of a Traveling Black Women: A Guide to International Travel

Mini Travel Guide Series

Dubai, Abu Dhabi & The 5 Other Emirates You Didn't Know About

Jamaica: Likkle, but Tallawah!

Studying Abroad for Black Women

Iceland: Nature, Nurture, & Adventure

Solo Travel: Try It At Least Once!

Teaching Abroad: From Abu Dhabi or Abuja

And more...

Contents

Preface

Many women grow up with the narrative that they have to go to school, meet a good man, get married to him, have children and then live happily ever after. Some of us want those things... but some also want more like traveling and living in exotic places around the planet. Why can't we have it all?

Well, my name is Kishema Malik and I'm better known as Pendu in the world that I belong to--dance and entertainment. I have been a professional dancer for most of my life. Dance has allowed me to travel to many exciting places around the world and even live in certain areas for up to three months. I have had the experience of living in three countries for this amount of time and one of those countries is a place that I truly adore and could have stayed: Cape Town, South Africa.

Cape Town is a beautiful diverse city with the same amount of amenities as any large American city. There are so many different types of people making up the population. It is about 2 hours away from Johannesburg by plane and has more of a tropical climate ranging from 63°F (17°C) in the winter and 81°F (28°C) in the summer. Most of the Cape is composed of a mix of Dutch, French, Malay, English, Afrikaner and Xhosa (pronouned co-sa) lifestyles but the Xhosa people are who I had the most contact.

The word Xhosa has a distinct "clicking sound" in the beginning of the word that is hard to pronounce but the people are very excited to teach you how to make this sound. For some reason it never worked for me. It is to your benefit to try and learn some of the Xhosa language if you are going to be amongst these people for an extended period of time. I did learn some words and by being a Black person it did help me to blend in when going into certain areas that were not so pleasant.

After my 23 hour journey from Las Vegas to South Africa, my impression was "wow, its kind of like home!" With my hometown being Queens, New York City. I was slightly shocked at the familiar infrastructure, how much hustle and bustle I witnessed and unfortunately how many Europeans were in charge in an African country. I mean no disrespect to our European brothers and sisters but we all know South Africa has a complicated history of struggle and civil rights that many Africans from the diaspora can totally relate.

Once I got past noticing these things I was

just in awe, in awe because this was my very first time on the continent, the motherland, the home of all civilization.   I just had to take a moment to be thankful to be in a position to experience such amazingness. Before my travels began many asked me why I was going to South Africa for such a long time and how did all of this come about? There were so many questions pertaining to the actual travel such as do you need shots? A visa? Where will you stay? How will you get around? How long will be staying there? Aren't you afraid? How will you eat and what will you eat?   These are all questions that will be answered throughout this book with as much detail as possible.

My time in South Africa was eventful and very different from the typical holiday that most single Black women take. During the remaining time of my trip I did find the time to attend underground night clubs and bars in Observatory (I avoided the typical downtown nightclubs because that is nothing special for me), as well as cafes, bookstores and small shops in the area I was living.

My favorite part of my time in South Africa was giving a dance class to an entire group of children with AIDS through the organizaion I was with. I literally still do not have the words to explain the greatness of these beautiful souls. All of them were so positive, kind, light-hearted and genuine. Every single child was eager to learn and did their best at every single step given to them. All of the teachers set up a rotation with some teaching acrobatics, juggling, aerial and dance. The kids got to train like they were going to be part of a circus. I admired them so much and it taught me how we should be viewing life and living every moment as if it were your very last breath. We probably gave them a workshop that lasted between 3-5 hours and once we were done I found myself not wanting these kids to leave. The love and light that filled the room during this workshop was pure and I was never the same after experiencing this.

What to Know

"I HAD OTHER PLANS FOR MY LIFE. BUT GOD HAD OTHER PLANS FOR ME. GOD'S PLAN WAS FOR ME TO FIGHT IN THE POLITICAL LIBERATION FOR MY PEOPLE."

History:

The history in South Africa is very complicated. While apartheid ended 1994, the segregation and differences in economic status were still evident. Apartheid was a system of institutionalized racial segregation that existed in South Africa from 1948 and continued until around 1994. On one side of a street you could see beautiful structured houses and mansions and then directly across the street you could see an entire township that was poor and underdeveloped. It forced me to challenge my American view of poverty and the lived reality of South Africans in poverty. Although I recognize that South Africa has evolved since apartheid, it still concerned me to know that while some lived so lavishly, others lived in such extreme poverty. There was one day in particular when a friend was helping our group find our way around. She indirectly hinted to us that she did not know the area that we were staying in because it was considered a "white" area based on the development. After walking a few miles we found a cab that was willing to take all of us back to our house as well as take her back to her village. This day ended up being quite exciting and informative. We actually started talking about the drastic social economical differences between certain areas of South Africa and the corruption that wearied many South Africans.

The major ethnic groups of South Africa include the Zulu, Xhosa, Bapedi, Venda, Tsonga and Swazi, all which predominantly speak Southern Bantu languages. Bantu is a term covering languages from Niger-Congo, which are spoken in central and southern Africa and include Swahili, Xhosa and Zulu.

The term Bantu also relates to the most widespread group of people in Africa. Around third century AD, the Bantu people gradually began to settle along the eastern coastline of Southern Africa. Some of the most populous Bantu tribes in Cape Town are the Xhosa people. Then, there is also a large population of the Zulu people in that area. The rest of the breakdown are the Coloured people, Asian/Indian, and White people.

When it comes to the label of *Coloured* people, those of African-American descent may think of the negative connotations that come with this word in American history. In South Africa, this term denotes a person of mixed race or heritage and were labeled as such because of the system of apartheid.

Airport Info:

Flying to South Africa is a full day event and depending on the airport your initial flight begins, it can be a two day event. I definitely recommend having a few books on hand, coloring books, some movie ideas to catch up on and if you sleep on planes, this would be a great time to catch up. My flight to South Africa went from Las Vegas to Washington, DC to Senegal, West Africa to Johanesburg, South Africa and then finally to Cape Town, South Africa. As long as you have enough time (2-3 hours) for your layovers, the trip will be smooth with minimal problems. Some problems that could arise are things like your luggage not making it onto the next flight if the layover's are not long enough or having to go through immigration and security again during a layover.

To fly into South Africa, you would most likely fly into one of two major cities: **Johannesburg** (O.R. Tambo International Airport - Airport Code: **JNB**) and **Cape Town** (Cape Town International

Airport - Airport Code: **CPT**).

Word to the wise... Johannesburg is usually the cheaper airport to fly into! You can always spend a few days and take cheap flight or travel on land to Cape Town from Johannesburg.

Visas:

Anyone living in the U.S. as a resident or citizen does not need to get a visa for South Africa (this was as of 2013 when I took my trip). US citizens and residents are allowed to travel to South Africa without a visa for up to 90 days for tourism or business purposes. I stayed for a little under 90 days so I did not have any trouble with entering or exiting South Africa. I am sure this still applies now in 2020, but I think it is always wise to check on the www.travel.state.gov website to verify before traveling.

Vaccinations:

The CDC has recommendations for travel vaccinations for South Africa but they are NOT required for entry. The vaccines recommended were Hepatitis A, Hepatitis B, Typhoid, Cholera, Yellow Fever, Rabies and Tetanus. I declined on all of the travel vaccines and did not get sick during my time there. I stayed almost 3 months.

On the other hand, I'm an advocate of doing what's best for YOU! Please go get the vaccines if you know you have a challenging medical history or even if it's just going to calm your mind. My decision was just my own personal choice. There is no wrong or right answer, but I definitely recommend that you what's best to make your travels as safe as possible.

Packing:

Cape Town, South Africa is mostly warm to hot with some rare occasions of it being a bit chilly. As stated earlier, Cape Town usually ranges from 63°F (17°C) in the winter and 81°F (28°C) in the summer and is very humid. Summertime in South Africa is NOT the same as summertime in the Western Hemisphere. Summertime begins in November and lasts until February. Winter on the other hand begins in late June until mid September.

I stayed in Cape Town from August until October 2013 and it was warm enough for me. That being said, it is best to pack for the weather as the weather patterns don't fluctuate often. I am a light packer and do not like traveling with a lot of luggage so if you are like me you can easily stay in South Africa for 3 months with just a duffle bag or small/meduim suitcase. However, if you are more lavish and like a lot of choices, then you may go to South Africa with one or two large suitcases. Some airlines will allow up to 2 free pieces of checked luggage.

While I would describe my experience in South Africa as safe, I would still recommend being mindful about your appearance as a tourist. You do NOT want the kind of attention that could lead to an unfortunate situation. The most fancy thing I brought was a simple sundress that I bought from Ross. I recommend bringing a lot of long flowing, simple sundresses as the culture there is more conservative than the typical America culture. It is best to show your legs and shoulders in moderation. I did very well wearing these dresses and would add a small cover up for my shoulders at times.

I would not recommend booty shorts, instead wearing jeans with a nice top is best. Honestly, my normal everyday wear while in South Africa was a pair of sweat pants and a baggy T-shirt. I preferred to look a bit plain and not attract any unwanted male attention.

I was in South Africa to teach and choreograph for the Zip Zap Circus. Our normal attire was usually dance clothing, sweats or yoga pants anyway!

I would also recommend carrying a smaller bag like a fanny pack or small backpack where you can keep cash (some areas do not take credit/debit cards) and a photocopy of your passport. You'll also want to make sure you always have your sunblock or bug repellant with you.

_____

_____

_____

_____

_____

_____

_____

_____

_____

_____

_____

_____

_____

_____

_____

_____

_____

_____

_____

_____

_____

_____

_____

Packing List

What to Expect

Being a Black Woman

Traveling in general to any country in the world has its ups and downs, but nothing that will make me want to ever stop traveling. Once you have a system and educate yourself about the destination, then everything else falls into place. In my experiences, the pros usually outweigh the cons. I was sent to South Africa to teach and choreograph for the Zip Zap Circus located in Cape Town, South Africa. They housed me in a home mixed with artists from the circus school and other foreigners who came to volunteer, teach or give time to this wonderful circus.

Zip Zap circus also took care of my flight details, housing and food while I was there for a small fee. The reason I am explaining this is because I had some basic things of life taken care of for me to help my trip be smooth and simple. How you plan your trip does affect the outcome of your trip--especially as a Black woman.

Even though apartheid was over in 2013 when I was there, people were still pretty segregated by choice. To be considered Black you had to be of a tribe, from another African country or just really dark skin with African features. I am an African-American/Caribbean woman of lighter complexion so they all kept calling me "coloured" even though I identify as being Black.

I took this as an opportunity to learn more about their culture as I realized that they were not being rude by describing me as "colored." They informed me that any other Black American with a similar complexion would probably have a similar experience that I had. This is something to keep in mind as the term colored has a deeply negative connotation in the American culture.

South Africans are quite frank and speak their mind and they will label you as they wish. It took me awhile to get used to but they were also open to hearing my perspective about being Black and how my lifestyle is day to day in the U.S. I continued to share with them that I am seen as only a Black woman in America despite my complexion.

Speaking of frank, you'll find that it is customary for a South African man to come up to you and say, "I want to marry you." Even though this was a bit weird and creepy to me I noticed that this was an apporach that seemed to express something like "I like you and want to take you out and one day I will marry you." Obviously, I can't say this is how every South African man will act but it happened quite often during my stay so I think its important to take note.

I want to go over some of the highs and lows of being a Black woman during the entire travel and stay in South Africa.

Let's start with the lows:

- The first low is that most locals assume you are rich once they know you are from the U.S. This can be frustrating to explain because you may be rich in comparison to many living there but they did not seem to understand how the middle class is set up in the U.S. and how you even got the opportunity to travel. With this being said, you may be a target for petty theft and robbery so making sure to dressing casually and blending in may be to your benefit.

- Next is the assumption that you have a husband. Some may directly ask "how are you allowed to do this trip?" Or simply, "where is your husband?" when asking a question at a market. Most people are conservative in South Africa so you have to be patient with their notion that a single Black woman must have a husband or companion to be traveling this far away.

- Finally, the way the South African women may perceive you as a Black American woman. I was never treated badly but I was questioned about my authenticity as Black woman vs. the label of "Coloured" that was given to me. I often dress and look like a woman who grew up on the continent of Africa but my mannerisms and personality are Western or American in nature. Many people did not know how to categorize me, especially the women so I was questioned quite often. Some would look at this as bad attention but I did not and actually made friends with the women who were just curious to understand my being.

Now the pros:

- The first pro is obviously being BLACK! Even though I was stressing that you should be cautious about your surroundings and your belongings this is just using your common sense as the caucasian people will never blend and are automatically seen as wealthy tourists. For a Black person, it is much easier to blend in with the community.

- Another pro is being a Black American. Even though the media shows us in a negative light at times, they also show us as strong, powerful and innovative. Some may think of you as athletes, celebrities, musicians, etc. and will look at you in a positive light. At times they want to talk to you just because they think you are someone famous. Once they find out your truth, a lot of the locals still want to befriend you because they know we come from a similar complicated history and may want to spark deep conversations with you.

- The local men will give you plenty of attention and how you react to them can give you more of it or less. Honestly, I enjoyed the attention for the most part and was able to get treated in nightclubs, coffee, events and other gatherings. This can be tricky as some men will give you that attention because they are just charming or they really want something in return, which can be unpleasant. I would advise you to deal with this topic based on the same street smarts and common sense that you would use in your own country or state.

Humanity was born in Africa.
All people, ultimately, are African.

Cultural Norms

The culture in South Africa is a mix of western ways, conservative views, some Islamic beliefs and tribal customs of the native people. In some places you can move around similarly to how you would in America, while in others you'll want to be more conscious of the cultural norms. It really just depends on the area that you are spending time.

It is also customary to learn how to greet everyone in the local languages of the area even though everyone speaks English. It is typical for most South Africans to speak 7-9 languages without any hesitation! Since I was staying in Cape Town in an area called Observatory, the main tribe of people there were called the Xhosa people.

The Xhosa people speak Xhosa. The other tribes in this area include: Zulu, who speak Izizulu, coloured people *(FYI: The term "coloured" is **not** the same as we define it here in America as their history gives it a different meaning),* and the Afrikaans people who descended from the Dutch and Huguenot settlers of the 17th century.

Khayelitsha

As time progressed with working at the circus school we also did a lot of social justice work with local schools and went to various townships in Cape Town. This was very inspiring and humbling experience. It wasn't fair to see such extreme hardships between the rich and poor individuals living in such close quarters.

One of the biggest townships in Cape Town that I got to visit was named *Khayelitsha*--located in Western Cape on the Cape Flats. The name *Khayelitsha* is Xhosa for "our new home." *Khayelitsha* had varied levels of poverty within its township from some living in homes made of aluminum tin to some having a small typical house. Some locals tried to explain to me that there are lots of other complicated issues and politics surrounding why this was so.

After driving around and taking in the township, we went to a school to teach a circus perfomance class. It was a basic class of dance movement, acting and acrobatics. All of the children were very appreciative of our class and welcomed us to their community. We took a small walk around the township and saw that mostly everyone was friendly and welcoming. Although, I wouldn't suggest just going there without a local connection, I highly suggest learning about the

Xhosa people and how they live to erase any misconceptions that you may have had about South Africa. Many media outlets will tell you that it is so dangerous in *Khayelitsha* and that no foreigner should visit townships. That is not true, especially for us women of color.

This day came to an end with hugs from the children and packing up the circus van to return back to rehearsals at work. I know going to a township is not something usually planned for a vacation or holiday for most people but I do highly recommend going if you have time and really want to understand the true people of Cape Town. There was such a great disparity between the white people and black people in this country that it will make you think about the echoes of life beyond the American border.

"Now Now"

When someone says when "I'll be there 'now now,'" that really means like 10-15 minutes from the current time and "now" is like 5 minutes from the time you are standing in. Basically I learned the hard way that nothing really starts on time like we may be used to in the U.S., they are way more chill with time and feel like western people are too uptight and stressed about time.

I had the impression that since I was teaching and choreographing with an important show that time would be a factor. But even for important jobs, shows, meetings, events, everything always started 5-10 minutes late and it was totally normal for everyone.

Naming

One of the cultural norms that I loved is that the people you will be spend time with daily will name you in their language as a sign of endearment and fully welcoming you into their culture. Since I go by my middle name "Pendu," they took that name and made it South African. I was named "DuDuzile" which meant comforted in the Zulu langauge. I truly loved that gesture and hearing someone with a South African accent say my name makes me feel like I am back in this amazing country all over again.

Braai

One thing that is super customary and a lot of fun was going to what the South Africans call a *Braai*. *Braai* is an Afrikaans word that means barbecue or roast. It is similar to what we call a BBQ or cook out. In a *braai*, they take their meat and grill it on the grill over the fire with various spices and sauces, while they dance, drink, talk and plain out party while the fire remains lit for the duration of the night. Since I am a vegan they wrapped some vegetables up for me and grilled those over the fire so I could take part in this cultural event. People are happy, playing music, dancing to music and enjoying each other's company. Sometimes a braai goes on all night long as South African people know how to party.

When I asked why grilling this meat was such a big deal, many of them said it was because they do not eat a lot of meat as a culture because it is expensive. Therefore, during the normal part of the week they almost eat like I do, vegan!!!

I learned that the "vegan" terminalogy at the time was not popular in South Africa even though I found a number of their dishes to be vegan-friendly. Maybe now in 2020, this language may seem more normal and possibly a slight cultural norm for some of the younger community.

Tea Time

I loved drinking tea, specifically Roobois tea. Roobois tea, which means "Red Bush," is a broom-like member of the plant family Fabeceae that grows in South Africa's fynbos. The leaves are used to make this herbal tea. I feel like every liquid that I drank was tea. We would drink roobois tea for breakfast, we would have tea during breaks, tea for lunch and for dinner. I love drinking tea and if you love it too then you will have no problems in South Africa as they are some serious tea drinkers.

Being Vegan in South Africa

Eating was not a problem for me as a vegan in South Africa. A person native to South Africa typically does not eat meat every single day like they would in the U.S. When I explained I have been vegan since birth and it was all I knew, many began to make popular dishes that did not include meat for me. The South African cusine included many dishes that were vegan friendly. Some of these dishes included: Pap and chakalaka, plantains, yams, greens and other vegetables.

Restaurants were very accomodating. There were many locations that had diverse cuisine like Indian, Chinese, Ethiopian, Thai and more. Two restaurants that I remember going to were called *Plant* and *Raw and Roxy*. *Plant* had typical western cusine including burgers, nachos, sweet and cakes while *Raw and Roxy* had the raw food experience that was all an uncooked menu and geared to the super, heatlhy vegan.

South African Dishes

Many of the popular South African dishes included meat as well as some vegetable dishes that were just delicious. Meat eaters will love some of these popular dishes which include, Biltong and droewors (beef), Cape Malay curry (Indonesian decent), Chakalaka and pap (vegetarian dish made from onions, tomatoes, peppers, carrots, beans along with pap--a porridge similar to grits) and more. It is known that many of these dishes taste better at a local "mom and pop" shop than a commercialized restaurant.

Getting Around

I n the year 2013, Uber and Lyft did not exist yet and getting around in South Africa was definitely not by this mode. There were rideshares or vans called *kombis*, that usually had 16 seats and were used by about 60% of the population back then. They were often seen as dangerous because they would pack more people than number of seats. Another downfall to these *Kombis* is that you should NOT ride in one at night or in certain areas as a foreigner as pickpocketting and petty theft is not uncommon. Using the same judgement you would use in any major city is suggested if you want to experience traveling like a local.

A benefit to these rideshares is that they are cheap. Although I do feel that taking the kombis gave me a raw and authentic feeling living in South Africa. Now, you can find Lyft, Uber and other rideshare apps that are local to South Africa as a choice of travel.

Rideshare

Rideshares in 2013 compared to 2020 is drastically different. Cape Town still uses the local, traditional *Kombis* but now you have more of a choice and can change up your level of luxury.

- **Blacklane**
  - Blacklane connects riders to professional chauffers via their mobile app and website. Their fleet of cars include Mercedes E and S class, BMW, Lincoln Town cars, etc.

- **Bridj**
  - Bridj is a shuttle bus service that started off as American based then closed but now they offer serivce in a few countries including South Africa. Bridj differs from other rideshares as riders can request a seat on a shuttle bus along with other passengers heading in the same direction using the app. It's super affordable as prices range from $2 to $6 USD but may require the rider to walk a few blocks to catch the bus instead of door to door service.

- **Bolt**
  - Anyone wanting a private car but not as high in luxury can use the compa-

ny *Bolt*, which is similar to most ride-shares services in that your driver will be a local member of the community.

- **Uber**
  - Yes, Uber is available. It has many levels from basic 4 car sedans to luxury cars. It works the same just as if you were home in your country.

Trains

Trains are another way to get around if you need to travel to far distances from city to city or to another neighborhood. I still advise being smart and safe as you would at home.

During my trip I may have taken the train twice. The railway system in Cape Town is mainly focused on commuter transport but the Southern Line Rail Route is highly recommended for visitors. It stretches from Cape Town to Simon's Town and stops at several beautiful suburbs along the way. Most train travel was not always on schedule, so it's important to keep this in mind for whatever you have planned that day.

The other frequently used rail system is called the Metrorail Western Cape, which services most of the metropolitan area of Cape Town and surrounding towns of Malmesbury, Paarl, Stellenbosch, Wellington and Western Cape of South Africa.

Cape Town to Johannesburg

There are about 20 direct flights from Cape Town to Johannesburg that are under $100 USD, which is typically a good price between these two cities. It's about a 2-hour flight.

Climate

South Africa's climatic conditions generally range from Mediterranean in the southwestern corner of South Africa to temperate in the interior plateau and subtropical in the northeast. There is a small area in the northwest that has a desert climate but most of the country has warm, sunny days and cool nights. I did state earlier that the seasons are reversed for someone who is used to living in the Western hemisphere, the summer is during the months of November to January and their winter months are during June - August. I was shocked that sometimes their winter temperatures could reach freezing at high altitudes (and there are a lot of very high mountains) but when it gets cold its usually equivalent to a cold fall day in the US.

South Africa also experiences a high degree of sunshine with average rainfall increasing from west to east, and with semi-desert regions in the north to west. It would be wise to bring an umbrella if you visit during their fall or winter, but I did not bother with it as I did not mind getting my hair wet! :-)

Staying Connected

During my time in South Africa, I got used to NOT having my cell phone all the time the way I do when I am home. I got used to logging into their network at night time when I got home. Back in 2013, everyone in the house had to take turns being online, maybe 2-3 of us at a time because the signal was more fragile than what we were used to as Westerners. Even when there were not too many people logged in at once you still would have to be super close to the modem or the signal would still be dodgy.

You will also have to plan your day around not having typical phone service all day. Some things you will not have access to without your phone are GPS, your email while on the go, apps such as Facebook or other social media platforms that need internet to operate. Honestly, the only reason I had my phone with me was to have a camera to take pictures and video but other than that it was just a gadget sitting in my purse.

I planned my day by setting any need for

communication at night when I was done with work. Once you make a plan and a schedule to be online you can actually make a system to make you feel like you are still just as connected as you would be if you were home, it just takes proper planning.

Another way to get online is to go to an internet cafe where you can pay for a certain amount of time to get online and visit as many sites as you wish. Another option for connection was to use a calling card, which still may be a thing in 2020 unless you have international service on your phone.

I would definitely research options for the specific area that you will be in as there are some parts of the country that may not be as connected as others. Staying in contact overall was not a hard thing to do and I would say that even with the barest minimun of technology there are still so many ways to keep in touch with your loved ones when you are really far away. My method of communication was FaceTime so I felt like I was in normal communication as if I were still in the US during my time in South Africa.

2020

It's amazing how much technology can change in only seven years. I keep in touch with my South African friends and hear that their WIFI connectivity has increased 10-fold. In these current times the company COX provides most of the connectivity. The only down side is the WIFI is super expensive and still not accessible to many locals in South Africa.

Those staying in a resort or hotel situation would probably have the easiest access to fast WIFI than those staying in a hostel or AirBnB.

What to Do

S outh Africa itself has infinite things to see, experience, witness and participate in. It is just the most magical place. My time was mostly spent in Cape Town. I took road trips to Simon's Town, Robben Island and False Bay and many attractions surrounding the beautiful city of Cape Town. It was truly breathtaking.

Cape Town

C ape Town has a number of beautiful attractions and I had the pleasure of visiting many of them, though not all of them. I will go into detail about my experiences in each. The notable attractions I will be highlighting are:

- Boulders Beach
- Cape of Good Hope
- Cape Agulhas
- Khayelita
- Kirstenbosch National Botanical Garden
- Lion's Head
- Robben Island
- Simon's Town
- Table Mountain National Park
- Victoria & Alfred Waterfront

FYI, this will probably be the longest and most intense section of this book because my experiences going to most of these attractions were exciting, life changing, adventurous and some outright DANGEROUS!! You will understand what I mean when I get into detail but one thing I will warn anybody when visiting South Africa is that South African people love life and live life to the fullest. Even if that fun includes some danger, they will partake without hesitation. My experiences were not monitored by any tour guide because I was not there on a long holiday. I went to many locations with local people who live this kind of life daily. I will definitely say that your experience may not match mine if you are visiting and attending attractions with a formal tour guide. Either way, I am sure you will get to take in the beauty that is South Africa.

Once I got used to the time difference, which was 9 hours ahead for me, I was bombarded by my housemates to visit EVERYTHING! They wanted to show me so much with such great excitement that I had to remind them that I would be around for a few months and that we had time. With much enthusiasm the first place they wanted to take me was to hike a mountain called "Lion's Head."

Lion's Head

When you take an aerial view of the mountain it looks like an actual Lion's head, hence the name. I didn't realize how popular hiking was to South African people until they took me on this journey. For one, I didn't realize how high this mountain was at all until someone told me that we would be back home by evening. My reaction was "What??? Where exactly are we going and why will we be gone for so many hours?" One of my housemates just said that it would take about 2 hours to climb one way because it is 669 meters high. In my head that did not translate as much until I did the math and found that it equated to 2,194 feet!!! *OH MY GOODNESS* was all I could keep saying and felt like this was going to be a crazy day. The locals assured me that it won't be that bad and it would just be a nice hike and there will be a surprise when you get to the top. Needless to say, on the way to the top, I realized that this was way more than just a simple hike.

The day we all decided to hike I was still getting acclimated to being 9 hours ahead and the idea of being in Africa! My trip to South Africa was my first time being on the motherland continent EVER and I was very emotional everyday. Even though my roots are West African and not South African, just being in Africa was pure amazement.

All of these emotions came with me on my first hike to Lions Head.

On this day, I packed food, water and my phone to be used as my camera. Everyone was just casual and acting like it was going to be a nice stroll. I remembered them reminding me to wear very good shoes......that didn't register until later on.

All of us in the "Obs house" (my home in Observatory, Cape Town for the time I was there) got into the house van and drove to Lions head. On the way, I was just loving all of the rich nature, the mountains, the architecture, the flow of the city and the vibes all around me, it was so mesmerizing.

We probably drove about 30 minutes to get there. I noticed that people seemed to drive without obeying the rules of the road. Almost as if the rules were just to not crash into anything or anyone. As long as you did that, it seemed, you may go as fast as you want. It was a pretty crazy drive, but the driver seemed to have a handle on the way traffic flows in Cape Town so I tried to not worry too much and just enjoy the ride.

After this exciting ride we arrived at Lions Head, parked, got our things and started on our way. Of course me and the other foreigners had to start with taking pictures as we were already high up overlooking the city and all of the amazing nature and just the height of these mountains amazed me, just WOW! After we were done "modeling" with the most amazing scenery we started to walk. I remember thinking, "This is nice!" as we strolled on the dirt road as the mountain started to slightly incline. As the incline continued we continued to walk and of course we were told to stay with the group no matter what. Doing that was not as easy as you think. Many of us wanted to stop and take pictures as we walked, so we had to figure out how to get amazing photos but not stop the group. I managed to find my pace with keeping up with the group but still managed to get some epic photos with me displaying the body language "I'M IN AFRICA, YES!!!!"

Things started to get difficult because about a half an hour into the hike we started having to climb up using our arms. We went through these little obstacles and we just kept going higher and higher. I thought to myself, "Are we hiking or are we rock climbing?" Haha! Pretty soon we had to use more strength and even though I was strong enough to do this I kept thinking "How is this a damn hike though?" I thought a hike was just a nice walk through nature or on an incline of a mountain but not literally climbing a mountain!

We continued to climb, go through parts of the hike where we would have to pull ourselves up like we were in some obstacle course, we had to go up these metal type stairs, climb up to go down to just go back up again and it got vigorous!

After these obstacles I started to feel like, "OK this is just enough, what are we doing?" I let the group know that I was starting to become very uncomfortable and was getting super anxious but the group kept telling me that we must stay together and we could not split up now. Splitting up would be more dangerous because there was no actual tour guide.

At this point of the journey I really felt emotional and defeated like this was bad idea. At the same time the surroundings and the feeling of being in Africa were greater and managed to keep me going. So, with every step and climb I took a deep breath and I only looked up as we continued this trek to the top of Lions Head. After a little over 2 hours, we got up to the top of Lions Head. I felt like I won a million dollars and found myself releasing tears of joy.

The group started yelling "LOOK!" and when I looked, what I saw gave me chills. The "gift" that was waiting for us at the top of this mountain was the clear visual of **Robben Island**. The island that housed the prison that Nelson Mandela was locked away in for 27 years! Later on I will talk about my trip to Robben Island and visiting his actual cell.

Seeing this view was astonishing! It was like we were on top of the world, seeing Robben Island, seeing all of the mountains surrounding us, seeing the homes, the magical ocean and beautiful birds soaring in the sky. It was picture time all over again and since we were circus people, we took images in handstands, balancing on one leg, goofy shots and then one last group shot. The happiness around us was life changing and made me feel like I was truly living without restriction.

Once this was done we all took a moment to ourselves in whatever peace each person believed in and started to pack up for our descent down Lions Head. Now, this descent was not physically hard but it was more dangerous because of the steepness. We took our time going downwards with most of us actually sitting and sliding down very carefully. I laughed because I could not believe that I was afraid of going up, which was physically harder but going down was clearly more dangerous! I would say that we took a good hour to an hour and 15 minutes to get down because we were going so slowly. Once we made it to the bottom, we felt relieved and invigorated as if we accomplished something very big. We laughed and chatted our way to the car and got ready to go to our home for a great dinner as a household. Once we got back we just talked about the adventure and how crazy climbing a mountain that high was for the foreigners while the locals kept insisting that it wasn't a big deal. This is just an example of how cultures vary and how something safe to one person can seem super dangerous to another. Our next venture as a household luckily didn't involve anything scary or strenuous.

My main reason for being in Cape Town was to teach and choreograph for the Zip Zap circus school. I was pretty lucky that the host of the school made it an important part of my total experience to take me and the other housemates on excursions and fun adventures to make sure we got the best feel for South Africa.

There was so much that I still did not get to experience, but the one thing that I couldn't wait to do was go to the beach! Cape Town is known for having some of the prettiest beaches in the world!

Boulders Beach

After a couple of weeks working at the Zip Zap circus it was definitely time for us to have a break and I could not wait to go the beach. We went to a few beaches but the one beach that was special was called Boulders Beach. Boulders Beach is a sheltered beach made up of inlets between granite boulders and is located in the Cape Peninsula near Simon's Town (another attraction that we went to and we'll visit later).

This beach is commonly known as Boulders Bay and its a popular tourist attraction because of a colony of African penguins which settled there in 1982. Only a few of us went on this trip and it was super calm, chill and relaxing. We witnessed the beauty of the crisp, blue water and wind blowing us around with so many rocks surrounding us. Across from this beach were lots of shops, restaurants, bars and just an active tourist spot for many to enjoy before or after visiting this lovely beach. This beach is a paying beach but it's worth the small fee to spend the day in Cape Town's best swimming area. I remember going with only 3 of my French roommates and one South African girl who was almost like my little sister, so there was no urgency of an itinerary that usually surrounds a big group. Since we were circus people we did a lot of balancing on rocks handstands, cartwheels and just being big kids on the sand.

Then, we finally saw the cute penguins that this beach was known for. The African penguins waddled in groups and chilled on the rocks while some splashed around at the edge of the water. I thought that they were the cutest things and just kept taking pictures of them. I noticed Lion's

Head in the background of many of my photos. Everything felt so connected. A local passing by informed me that Boulders Beach actually forms part of the **Table Mountain National Park,** which is across from Lion's Head so my pictures continued to have the memorable image of Lion's Head to remind me of my hike.

We let the day linger and just enjoyed the fresh air and beautiful scenery of this beach. Afterwards we took a long walk and tried to find a cab to go home. We actually got a little lost. My cell phone was non-existent as I left it at the house. The same applied to my friends that came with us. Lucky for us we did not go totally alone and had our South African connection who knew the area pretty well. She reminded us that Cape Town is big and that where she lives is no where near where we were.

Table Mountain National Park

Table Mountain is a major tourist attraction in Cape Town. With stunning views of Cape Town, it is another must - see destination. At its highest point, Table Mountain is 1,085 meters above sea level! Some choose to hike (clearly Lion's Head was enough for me), but most take the famous Aerial Cable Car. There are also guided plateau walks (not hikes) that lead you to gorgeous views. The walks range from 15 minutes in length to about 40 minutes. As a part of the Cape Floristic Region, Table Mountain is home to thousands of plant species that you will not find anywhere else in the world.

And, as with any touristy place, there are tons of shops and restaurants (with beautiful views) to explore.

Simon's Town

Another location that was enjoyable was called Simon's Town--about an hour drive from Cape Town. We were driven by a lovely gentle-men that also worked at the circus school. This was a nice trip because we did not have to rely on taxi's, trains or any sort of public transportation.

Simon's Town felt safe and has one of the lowest crime rates in the country. Traveling as a

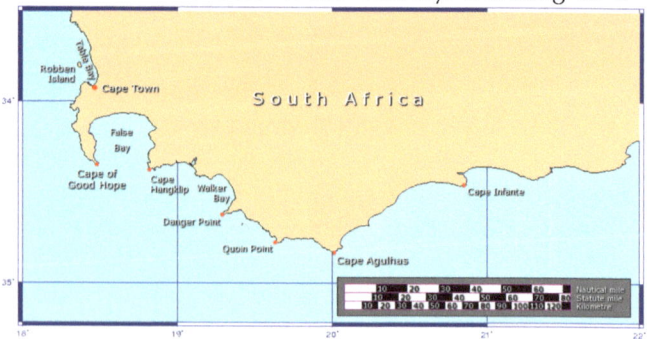

Map By Johantheghost - Own work, CC BY-SA 3.0, https://commons.wikimedia.org/w/index.php?curid=541146

solo Black woman should be fine. Some people ask, so what's so amazing about Simon's Town? Due to its location on the shores of False bay, the amusement of Simon's Town is whale watching! The best time to do this is usually from the months of June to November but you can still can see these whales at any time of the year. The area is fascinating with lots of mountainous images, clear waters, lots of shops and cafes and lots of rocks situated in the ocean high enough to sit and watch the whales. As long as you have a lot of patience you could see many types of whales or even a family of them. I may have seen about 8-10 whales during my visit. To optimize your whale watching time you want to go see the whales during the time slot between 11am and 3pm.

As the day went on we took more pictures, (of course) and ate at one of the local restaurants overlooking the ocean, which was quite beautiful. On the way back to Cape Town we stopped to witness the most beautiful landscape. We got out of our cars and did daring poses on the edge near the ocean (yes, I'm adventurous) as well as some more circus moves. After being circus weirdos :) we managed to get home safely to be ready for dinner as a household and get ready for work the next day.

Cape of Good Hope

After a few more weeks of work the next few scheduled trips involved going to Cape of Good Hope, Robben Island and to various malls and local shops that were selling authentic gear. I chose for us to take our next trip to Cape of Good Hope because I thought it was the southern most tip of Africa, where the Atlantic Ocean meets the Pacific Ocean but I learned quickly from a local that this was a misconception.

The Cape of Good Hope was NOT the southern most tip of Africa! I was in shock and wanted to know why this was and by taking this trip we were going to find out this little mystery. As usual we figured out how were we going to get to our destination and once again we were lucky enough to have the help of one of the workers of the circus school to take us.

We took the ride, which was maybe 20-30 minutes long. When we got to the entrance of Cape of Good Hope, we noticed that there was a fee of 90 Rand ($15 - $18) per PERSON!!! We all were in shock and knew that this price could not be right. We thought that maybe they meant per car because its just an overlook at the beach, how could it be that expensive, right? As we pull up to the entrance, the person says "it will be 90 Rand PER PERSON please!!" Everyone in the car

looked at each other and decided that it was ridiculous to just look at the ocean for that price, even though we all could afford it. We felt that it was the principal of the whole thing so we asked where we could make a U-turn and leave. Sadly we left but then our friend Emmanuel who was always driving us told us "I can take you to the real point of Africa anyway." That comment excited us all!

Cape Agulhas

Our driver informed us that the *real* southernmost point of Africa was called Cape Agulhas. It was about 90 miles (150 km) southeast from where we were at Cape of Good Hope. All of us in the car started singing songs to thank our driver as this location was a good 2 hour drive. Once we arrived and parked we started to carefully walk around all of the rockiness and admiring the two oceans (Atlantic and Pacific) coming together, the REAL point of South Africa! I had many peaceful moments walking around this place and of course had to do some circus poses! During the drive back home we could not help but take more pictures of striking landscapes. It is just so beautiful.

Victoria & Alfred Waterfront

Anyone who loves good old shopping, sightseeing and just mingling should definitely take a trip over to VA Waterfront. VA stands for Victoria and Alfred Waterfront and is situated on the Atlantic shore, Table Bay Harbor, the City of Cape Town and Table Mountain. It's a wonderful place with great shops, cafes, and restaurants. The surroundings were epic and I was often able to see my favorite, the "South African Gumboot" dancers, performing for the public for donations.

South African Gumboots dance is native to South Africa. This dance originated in the mines, where the mine workers were being forced to work with little compensation and not allowed to speak. Hitting their boots became a means of communication and then turned into competitive games, which later became a dance. This dance has rich history and culture and can be seen anywhere in South Africa, especially at places like the V&A Waterfront.

I had such a good time walking around at this waterfront that I suggest going here at least twice. You do not need to bring a lot of money as you can just walk around, take in the scenery, watch the entertainment and soak up some vitamin D. Many westerners find a lot of comfort here as many commercial and popular stores that are in the US can be found here as well.

Hermanus

Hermanus is a resort town located on the Western Cape and is known for it's whale-watching crowd. There is a museum on-site that depicts South Africa's fishing and whaling history. Outside of whale-watching, Hermanus is also a nice place for wine-tastings, visiting the beach, and fine dining!

Robben Island

To get to Robben Island we had to return to VA Waterfront, where we were able to take more pictures and see things we did not see before. What made this tour extra special was that after you buy your ticket there was an entire tour around the building displaying the history of Nelson Mandela in great detail. It went through Mandela's earlier years, his history and why he was put in jail. There were even displays of just South African history relevant to Nelson Mandela to help get the broader scope of who he was. Mr. Mandela was a South African anti-apartheid revolutionary, political leader and philanthropist, who served as President of South Africa from 1994-1999. He went to prison in 1962 for conspiring to overthrow the state and was locked up for 27 years split between Robben Island, Pollsmoor Prison and Victro Verster Prison. We learned that Nelson Mandela did not go to jail alone as he was imprisoned with others, who were on the same mission.

After maybe a good hour of going through this area, it was time to get on the ferry boat to Robben Island for the remaining 2.5 hours of this tour. As we started to board the ferry I was excited to see what more was to come of this tour, especially seeing Nelson Mandela's jail cell. It took about 10-15 minutes to board the ferry as it could fit quite a few people on board, maybe up to 200 or more. The ride was about 32 minutes. This shocked me because the island was about 5 miles away and located in Table Bay with an amazing view of Table Mountain from Robben Island. It didn't look as far as it seemed and the wind resistance made us take a little longer to get there.

One memory that I will not forget was how rough this ferry ride was! We were going so fast and the water was splashing everywhere! It felt like there were moments that we were going to tip over or something. I even closed my eyes to try and nap through but that only lasted a few minutes. I kept wondering why the ferry was going so fast and why was it so rough! Once again, I saw that South Africans loved living on the edge just like we did on our hike on Lion's head!

We all made it safely to Robben Island and our journey felt like it was just beginning! Once they ferry arrived all of the passengers were split into 3 or 4 buses that took us around the entire island to see the prison, buildings, monuments and houses of the 116 inhabitants living there of which some were ex-prisoners from the prison.

The bus I rode started at the prison before driving around the island. Upon arriving at the prison you see an amazing wall painting that says "FREEDOM CANNOT BE MANACLED" which is another way to say freedom can't be shackled or chained. This walled painting represented the struggle that Nelson Mandela and other activist that were against apartheid believed in. Once we were done taking pictures with this mural the tour guide (some tour guides are actually ex-prisoners) escorted us all into the prison and started explaining history of the prison beginning in the courtyard.

The tour guide was explaining that this facility was not only a prison but it used to also be a post office, a grazing ground and a mental hospital. It was most well known for its use as a political prison and was closed after the fall of apartheid. The tour guide took us into the first area with only a bench, sink and barred windows. We were told that this area was used as a moving area for the prisoners or holding place for when they had to switch cells. It felt eerie and strange walking around this place as it felt haunted or had some kind of hovering spirits around us.

Next, we started walking to the area where they had gatherings where the prisoners could pray, fellowship and have some kind of social interaction. I found everything to be plain and dismal. In each room there were explanations and history given about the island, prison life, the prisoners and of course, Nelson Mandela. After this we went through another courtyard into another building with more dismal hallways. We went into the areas where the holding cells were located. The tour guide showed us how various cells were designed and set up. Most of them had a flat bed on the floor, a sink and a toilet. These cells were probably no more than 10 ft wide and 10 ft long, maybe smaller. After getting the information about other prisoners and each cell, we finally came to Nelson Mandela's cell.

Arriving at Nelson Mandela's cell was surreal as I have been reading and learning about him since I was a child. To see his history unfold right in front of our eyes was just unreal. As soon as we get to his cell the tour guide says "46664", which was Nelson Mandela's prisoner number stemming from him being the 466th prisoner on the island in

1964. To date, 46664 continues to be used as a reverential title for him.

Mr. Mandela's cell was just like the others, small, plain and eerie and made you respect this man even more to spend 27 years of life in a place like this. Once the tour guide was done talking about Nelson Mandela's cell and his history he allowed us to take photos of his cell then asked if there were anymore questions. Afterwards, he then had us head to the bus to take a tour of the rest of the island. As we got on the bus, the tour guide informed us that we would be driving slowly to see all of the elements of the island apart from the prison. The first stop was one of those souvenir shops where you can get snacks, go to the restroom, mingle with the other tourists and enjoy the amazing view. I loved that we could see more of those African penguins that were usually around Table mountain and various beaches around Cape Town. These penguins are the cutest things and tend to pop up around areas by water at any given time.

Once we were done taking pictures and talking with everyone we boarded the bus again to finish off the tour, which included seeing some of the architecture of the houses that were inhabited, the school they had on the island and the post office. This island was very quaint, quiet and seemed like a little oasis away from the mainland of Cape Town. After 3 hours the tour came to an end and the tour guide gave some last remarks and asked if we had any questions. We spent another 10-15 minutes with questions and answers and then got back on the ferry for the mainland. I must say that the trip back was more quiet than the ride on the way to Robben Island because most of us were EXHAUSTED! I will definitely say that a trip to Cape Town will not be complete until you take part in this tour to Robben Island!

Wine Tours

South African wine is as popular a wine as Italian, French, or Australian wine. Therefore, it was no surprise to see that South African Wine Tours in Cape Town came a dime a dozen. I knew that Cape Town had a bunch of amazing wine tours, but I did not go to any at all. Why? Honestly, it just wasn't a priority for me. I did so much in my time here that there just was no time! The wine tours are generally full day events that include a drive to a winery, a tour of the winery, a wine tasting, and a drive back to Cape Town City Central.

Luckily, I had friends and connections to fill me in on this topic as I know that most folks heading to South Africa on vacation would defi- nitely want to add a good wine tasting to the itinerary. Many of the best wineries are small family-owned wineries.

The following are wine tours and/or wine shops that are recommended:

1. Vaughan Johnson's Wine Shop at Market Square, V&A Waterfront

2. Steven Rom Exporters at Sea Point

3. Old Wine Shoppe at Mariner's Wharf, Hout Bay

4. The Wine Shop at Constania Uitsig, Spaanschemat River Rd, Constantia

5. Manuka Cafe and Fine Wines, Steenberg Village, Reddam Ave

6. Shop 9, Manuka Wine Boutique, Noordhoek Farm Village

7. Chenin Restaurant and Wine Bar, Waterkant St, De Waterkant

8. Caveau Wine Bar and Deli, 92 Bree St, Cape Town

9. LovaneE Boutique Wine Estate & Guest House *(Pictured)*

Sample Itinerary

My experience was more of a work position so I had many things included and/or taken care of because of my job. Therefore, my sample itinerary should be looked at very loosely as everyone's purpose for travel may not be the same. One more thing I want to add before sharing my sample itinerary is that where you stay for the time you are in South Africa will heavily affect your experience and day to day activities. Since I stayed in a communal house with locals and other expats I would say the next best thing to get a similar experience would be a hostel or a nice AirBNB. Hotel stays are nice as well but you may not get to be fully engulfed into the culture and way of life that the locals live. Nevertheless, just the fact that you are in this magical place you will have fun regardless.

A sample itinerary to me would be starting your day like a South African by drinking some Rooibos tea. Then, having a nice lunch and dinner at any of the local shops, cafes or restaurants.

After having dinner it is always nice to end the night at a lounge or small bar for a drink and nice music. I did not party a lot during this trip as

I tried to save my energy to teach all of the dance classes on my schedule.

Seven days in Johannesburg & Cape Town

- **Day One:** Arrive in Johannesburg

- **Day Two:** Full Day Tour including Soweto, Johannesburg, and the Apartheid Museum

- **Day Three:** Flight to Cape Town

- **Day Four:** Full Day Cape Town Wine Tour

- **Day Five:** Full Day Cape Town Culture Tour including Robben Island and School Visit in Langa

- **Day Six:** Full Day Cape Town Safari

- **Day Seven:** Depart Cape Town

Animal Safaris

An animal safaris in Cape Town is another "must-add" to your South African Itinerary. There are a number of safaris outside of Kruger National Park that provide a quality experience while ensuring the animals are safe in their environment.

There are many options for Safaris on game reserves that are likely to have the Big 5 (lion, leopard, rhino, elephant, buffalo). Aquila Private Game Reserve Safari & Spa, which is about a two hour drive from Cape Town, is highly recommended as it provides an excellent experience with a little complimentary champagne along the way! Tours generally include hotel pickup, lunch, and a guided tour around the reserve.

Nightlife

Cape Town has an amazing nightlife scene that will remind you of a city like New York, Los Angeles or Las Vegas. Some night clubs focus on local music, afro-beats and house and some play the typical top 40 music that you would hear in any US night club. I thought the parties in the townships and local lounges were better than the mainstream night clubs, but that could be because I am from New York and have lived in Los Angeles and Las Vegas. I wanted more authenticity.

The crowd you party with was also a factor as many of the black South Africans still separated themselves from the white South Africans, which always changed the vibe at any nightclub. Nightlife in Cape Town is not much different than that in any major city.

The Living Room

Cape Town has some of the same high-class night clubs that are in Los Angeles or New York that also includes that class of people that are more on the "bougie" side. A night club for a crowd like this would love going to "The Living Room." This is night club is a sophisticated, multi-level entertainment venue. They have a stylistic VIP lounge, cocktail bar, restaurant, cigar lounge and Dance arena. The Living Room has a strict dress code. Ladies have to wear heels and men have to wear suit gear. The music here is also very generic and Top 40. If you are into dancing hard like me, this may not be the scene for you. Like most clubs, they have a "right to refuse" policy so dress to impress.

Observatory

I spent most of my nights in Observatory, which is where I was living so I did not have to worry about commuting and traveling late. Some popular night spots in Observatory included:

- **Trenchtown** - Has a cute outdoor area
- **Stones** - Casual vibe with pool tables and drinks
- **Reservoir Lounge** - Cozy vibe and amazing music
- **Obz cafe** - Has the best coffee

There were many other spots in the area that I did not go to but I have to say that Observatory was super accommodating to the young, urban and hip crowd.

This brings me to some of the actual night clubs in the area and in downtown...

Long Street

Long Street in Cape Town is a major hub for nightlife! The street is lined with bars, pubs, lounges and restaurants. It is the perfect place for bar hopping or simply exploring different scenes. Long street is one of those lively areas in a city that has a little something for everyone!

Here are the top 5 spots for your partying pleasure:

DecoDance Night Club

The first spot that is a fun location for groups, people that like pool, people who like trance music, a casual atmosphere not far from the water and who look for a friendly LGBTQ crowd. Typically a 4 out of 5.

Fiction

This is another nightclub with a cool, contemporary late night bar feel. This club is in a cellar of an 150 year old building. This nightclub was also casual and friendly to the LGBTQ crowd as well. Another plus to this nightclub is that it is only a 3 minute walk to the Company's Garden Restaurant for some good food.

Coco

This club is popular for their amazing cocktails and finest commercial hip-hop, house and dance music. This club has a sexy, glam environment that has been designed by the country's hottest interior designer. Coco is also known to have excellent customer attention and high end bottle service.

ReSet

Lastly, a nightclub in the heart of Cape Town that has been renamed since I was there, is now called "Reset." They have a lot of free events here, and when you do have to pay, it isn't much. Drinks were cheap and the atmosphere was upbeat. They play hip hop, techno, deep house and anything that is high energy!

Johannesburg

Although my time was primarily spent in Cape Town. There are quite a few notable spots in Johannesburg that are worth the visit while in South Africa! Johannesburg is a bustling city with a rich history. Most of the most notable sights are historic in nature. If you are interested in visiting both Johannesburg and Cape Town on your trip, the recommendation would be to start in Johannesburg and then fly over to Cape Town.

With that said, here are the top three must-dos in Johannesburg.

- The Apartheid Museum
- Mandela House
- Guided Tour of Johannesburg

The Apartheid Museum

The Apartheid Museum offers permanent and temporary exhibits highlighting South Africa's turbulent history with segregation. If you are visiting South Africa, particularly Johannesburg and the surrounding cities, the Apartheid Museum is a must see.

The Mandela House

The Mandela House is actually owned by the Apartheid Museum. If you plan on visiting Robben Island in Cape Town, you'd definitely want to tour the Mandela House in Soweto. The Tutu House, home of Archbishop Desmond Tutu is also within walking distance.

Guided Tour of Johannesburg

Johannesburg, often referred to as Jo'burg, is a bustling metropolis that is worth a guided tour. South Africa has such a rich history that is worth exploring and Jo'burg is a great place to begin. Be sure that your guided tour includes Soweto, but be mindful of taking photographs of residents without their comfort or consent.

Diary

About the Author

Kishema Pendu Malik has been to over 33 countries because of her life as a professional dancer/instructor and choreographer. She loves traveling and just received her license as a luxury travel advisor in March 2020.

Kishema started to really travel in 2004 when she was offered a job to teach dance and fitness in Tulum, Mexico for 3 months. After that experience she was hooked on international travel. As a dancer, choreographer and instructor, Kishema's career took her to Brazil, Peru, Argentina, Sweden, Australia, all over Asia, Ghana and of course, South Africa.

She hopes to be an inspiration to many, especially women from neighborhoods like Far Rockaway, Queens, where she was born and raised until she was a teen. Many Black women from where she is from do not usually get the opportunity to travel the way she has traveled. As a result, she hopes her experiences help many to understand that anything is possible.

     Kishema also wants to inform and inspire other Black women with dietary restrictions. Kishema was born in a time where the word "vegan" was rarely being used but grew up on a totally plant-based diet. Eating internationally has never been a problem for her and quite frankly some of the best food she has tried has been out of the U.S.! Follow Kishema to learn more about her life abroad.

@pendudance
@afro_sexy

www.travelingblackwomen.com

www.ingramcontent.com/pod-product-compliance
Lightning Source LLC
Chambersburg PA
CBHW040856120626
46551CB00001B/36